MAUI
The Valley Isle

Written and Photographed
by
Allan Seiden

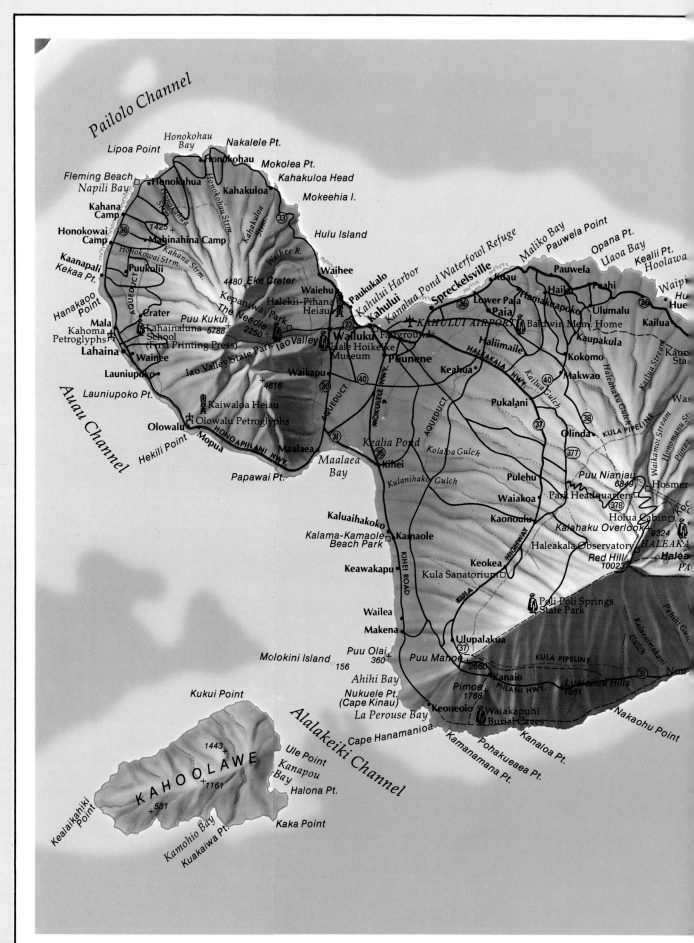

Pailolo Channel

Lipoa Point
Honokohau Bay
Nakalele Pt.
Honokohau
Mokolea Pt.
Fleming Beach
Napili Bay
Honokahua
Kahakuloa Head
Kahakuloa
Mokeehia I.
Kahana Camp
Honokowai Camp
Mahinahina Camp
Kaanapali
Kekaa Pt.
Puukolii
Hulu Island
Hanakaoo Point
Crater
Puu Kukui
Waiehu
Eke Crater
Waihee
Mala
Lahainaluna School
(First Printing Press)
Kahoma Petroglyphs
Lahaina
Wainee
Launiupoko
Launiupoko Pt.

Auau Channel

Olowalu
Olowalu Petroglyphs
Kaiwaloa Heiau
Hekili Point
Mopua
Papawai Pt.
Maalaea

Kepaniwai Park
The Needle
Halekii-Pihana Heiau
Iao Valley State Park
Iao Valley
Hale Hoikeike Museum
Waikapu

Paukukalo
Kahului Harbor
Kanalua Pond Waterfowl Refuge
Waiehu
Wailuku
Puunene
Keahua

Kahului
Kahului Airport
Fairgrounds

Spreckelsville
Lower Paia
Paia

Kuau
Haiku
Hamakuapoko
Baldwin Mem. Home

Maliko Bay
Pauwela Point
Pauwela
Opana Pt.
Uaoa Bay
Kealii Pt.
Hoolawa
Waipi
Hue

Ulumalu
Kailua
Kaupakula
Kokomo
Makawao

Maalaea Bay
Kihei
Kealia Pond
Kolaloa Gulch
Kulanihako Gulch

Kaluaihakoko
Kalama-Kamaole Beach Park
Kamaole
Keawakapu

Pulehu
Waiakoa
Kaonoulu
Keokea
Kula Sanatorium

Pukalani
Olinda
Puu Nianiau
6849
Park Headquarters
Hosmer

Haleakala Hwy.
Kula Pipeline

Holua Cabin
9324
Kalahaku Overlook
Haleakala Observatory
Red Hill
10023

HALEAKALA
Halea
PA

Poli-Poli Springs State Park

Wailea
Makena
Ulupalakua

Puu Olai
360
Molokini Island
156
Puu Mahoe
2660

Ahihi Bay
Nukuele Pt. (Cape Kinau)
La Perouse Bay
Keoneoio
Pimoe
1766
Kanaio
Waiakapuhi Burial Caves

Kula Pipeline
Luaalaha Hills
1981
Kanaloa Pt.
Kamanamana Pt.
Pohakueaea Pt.
Kanaloa
Piilani Hwy.
Nakaohu Point

Cape Hanamanioa

Kukui Point

Alalakeiki Channel

KAHOOLAWE
1443
1161
581

Kealaikahiki Point
Ule Point
Kanapou Bay
Halona Pt.
Kaka Point
Kamohio Bay
Kuakaiwa Pt.

Louis Louie

TABLE OF CONTENTS

Map labels:
maui Pt.
Honomanu Bay
Keanae Pt.
Keanae
Wailua
Wailua Bay
'ark
Nahiku
Puaa Kaa Falls State Park
Kalahu Point
Piilanihale Heiau
HANA AIRPORT
Honomaele
Waianapanapa State Park
Kaeleku
Nanualele Pt.
Heleiekoha Stream
Hana Bay
mpground
Kaahumanu Birthplace
d Loop
akauhi
Hana
Pohaku Palaha
+8105
Alau I.
ONAL
Paliku Cabin
Hamoa
Waiohonu Strm.
Mokae Cove
Waihoi Valley
alaoa Cabin
Wailua Falls
Puuiki
Kipahulu Valley
Haou
Kaupo Gap
Muolea
Aleile Stream
Koali
Muolea Pt.
DUCT
Kanekauila Heiau
Wailua Cove
Seven Sacred Pools
a Heiau
Puhilele Point
Kipahulu
Mokulau
Kaupo
Kailio Point
Manalu Bay
Petroglyphs
le Pt.

Alenuihaha Channel

0   5   10
STATUTE MILES

Molokini Island
acts as a natural sanctuary, teaming with a variety of marine life.

A rainbow of color filters through the fronds in a group of palms. The hula provides a subtle introduction to the beauty of Maui's Polynesian past. While there's no pressure to do anything more strenuous than relax on the beach, sparkling waters provide their own irresistible temptation.

Maui

AN INTRODUCTION

A stunning combination of lush mountains, stark volcanic craters, gold to white sand beaches, and luminous tropic seas provide Maui with an everpresent natural beauty. But more than the obvious attractions make Maui what it is, for its beauty is matched by the heartfelt aloha of its people, a long and varied history, and an imaginative range of attractions and activities designed to take advantage of all that Maui has to offer. Throw in a steady supply of clear skies and ample doses of sunshine, and it's easy to understand the saying *"Maui no ka oi,"* Maui is the best.

While tourism has only recently begun to play a significant role in shaping Maui's future, the impact of change has already been considerable. Today Maui welcomes visitors with four planned destination resorts that have helped to set the standard worldwide. Kaanapali Beach, Kapalua, Wailea, and Makena, as well as a large number of independent hotels and condominiums along a thirty-mile stretch of coast — running from Kihei and Maalaea in the east to Honokawai, Kahana, and Napili in the west — provide a range of accommodations rivaling those anywhere in the world.

In Hawaii, where by ancient tradition the land is considered sacred, resorts have been designed to harmonize with the setting rather than overwhelm it. More often than not, the results have successfully combined the casual with the sophisticated. It is not inaccurate to say that Mauians love their island, or that profit is rarely the sole consideration when it comes to making use of its many assets. For most of those who live here, Maui is the ultimate escape, and few would care to go farther afield in search of an alternative that could so justly be called paradise.

Imagination has been the key to successfully opening Maui to the growing number of visitors who have made it Hawaii's most popular neighbor island. While there's no pressure to do anything more strenuous than relax on the beach, numerous exciting activities provide more than a casual temptation to explore. Cruises depart Lahaina and Maalaea harbors daily, ranging from hour-long whale-watches to day sails to nearby Lanai. Snorkeling, scuba, windsurfing, Hobie cat sailing, Boogie boarding, sport fishing, parasailing, and jet skiing each lure their share of novices and enthusiasts.

Options for landlubbers are just as varied and include eight exquisitely situated and beautifully maintained golf courses, numerous tennis courts, stables for horseback riding, and downhill cycling (try the thirty-eight mile trip from Haleakala's summit to the coast). In addition a variety of van and motorcoach tours range from the Haleakala sunrise to all-day excursions to Hana.

From the air Maui presents additional spectacles, with helicopter tours of Haleakala, the dramatically eroded West Maui Mountains, and Hana, as well as excursions by helicopter or plane that tie in neighboring Molokai.

History has also left its imprint on Maui, providing an assortment of activities ranging from a ride on Hawaii's only remaining narrow-gauge cane railroad, to visiting fully restored missionary homes, to discovering ancient Hawaiian petroglyphs. Whatever your style, Maui is likely to provide indelible memories giving personal meaning to the saying "*Maui no ka oi*" . . . Maui is the best.

*P*alms grace the 14th hole of the Royal Kaanapali North Course, one of eight exquisitely situated and beautifully maintained courses on Maui. Snorkelers float in tropically lustrous seas. Maui offers Hawaii's greatest concentration of tennis courts and gardens.

*Iao Needle rises
1,200 feet from the heart of the
deeply eroded West Maui Mountains.
Three boys share a smile at
upcountry's Ulupalakua Ranch.
Pincushion protea, one of several
exotic flowers commercially grown
at upcountry nurseries, await
shipment to destinations
around the world.*

The island of Maui
was formed by the merging of ancient
lava flows from its two great
volcanoes, now-dormant Haleakala
and extinct West Maui.

An Island Is Formed

The great mid-Pacific range of volcanic mountains whose summits surface the ocean as the Hawaiian Islands, have been spewing forth vast amounts of lava for some 25 million years. Maui itself was formed by the merging lava of two great volcanoes, Haleakala and West Maui. Haleakala is by far the larger of the two, ranked as one of the most massive mountains on earth, its volume exceeding that of Mount Everest by more than fifty times. Haleakala's creation is the result of volcanism that in all likelihood is not yet completed, for silent Haleakala is considered dormant, not extinct.

The last eruption of this second largest island of the Hawaiian archipelago was a small event about two hundred years ago producing a coastal cinder cone that helped form La Perouse Bay. About the same time there was also volcanic activity within the summit depression known as Heleakala Crater.

Now peaking at 10,023 feet, Haleakala was once several thousand feet higher than it is today. Sometime in its prehistoric past, pressures built suddenly and a portion of the summit was blown away. Then erosion set in, and the same cumulative power that saw lava flows build this island, saw wind, rain, waves, and a powerful sun begin to undermine and wear it away.

Even the recurring ice ages directly influenced events. At their peak, when a growing icepack drained the seas of great volumes of water, sea level in the vicinity of Hawaii fell hundreds of feet. West Molokai, Lanai, and Kahoolawe, each separate volcanic islands, were thus joined to Haleakala and West Maui by vast lava valleys that had once been below sea level. This enlarged island is today referred to as Maui Nui, or Great Maui, in recognition of the fact that it was more than three times larger than Maui is today.

The process of Maui's explosive birth and monumental growth has only recently come to be understood. According to current theory, the Hawaiian Islands rise above a cluster of hot spots in the central Pacific that puncture the Pacific plate, one of a number of huge continental plates riding atop the more plastic layer of the earth's interior called the asthenosphere. As the plate moves over a hot spot, an island is formed as liquid rock, called magma, flowing upward from great underground reservoirs, reaches the surface, spilling out in great lava flows.

But simple volcanics are not all that is happening, for the entire archipelago is also in motion. Anchored to the Pacific plate like barnacles to the hull of a ship, the Hawaiian Islands are being carried by their host toward Japan at the rate of four inches a year.

Each island stays volcanically alive only as long as it maintains links to the magma below. When the northwest movement of the Pacific plate carries a volcano past the underlying hot spot, it becomes dormant, then extinct. Then settling begins and the process of growth is followed by slow but inevitable collapse. Not only does its very weight press each volcano back into the Pacific plate, but uninterrupted eons of wind and rain, of crashing waves and flowing streams, reduce the island's very substance. In time only a remnant remains, a great volcanic island surviving as a rocky pinnacle or coral atoll, eventually surrendering to the sea, hidden from sight as a submarine seamount. All this has already happened to the Hawaiian Islands that lie to the west of Kauai and Niihau.

Maui, however, lies to the east of Kauai, with dormant Haleakala bordering the cluster of hot spots that feed magma to the active volcanoes of the neighboring island of Hawaii. Lying one step farther removed from a source of subterranean magma, West Maui ceased erupting long ago and is therefore considered extinct.

The difference in appearance between Maui's two volcanic halves can be explained in part by this distinction between dormant and extinct. Even as Haleakala continued to grow, West Maui's fires died and erosion carved ragged contours into the curving symmetry of its original volcanic dome. Pounding waves shaped an alternating seascape of coastal cliffs and fine-grained beaches, while swift streams and waterfalls etched deep valleys between the sawtooth West Maui Mountains. The resulting spectacle includes geologic oddities like Iao Needle and expansive beaches like Kaanapali.

Only on Haleakala's west and south flanks and within its summit crater has erosion had the time to remake the landscape as on West Maui. The rest of this great mountain still has the unbroken surface of a potentially active volcano. Largely uneroded, Haleakala today accounts for more than three-quarters of Maui's 725 square miles of beauty.

From a seaside glimpse of West Maui's exquisitely mountainous core to the view from Haleakala's crater rim with the rest of the world lying below the clouds, from the warm and fragrant breeze that rustles through a Hana rain forest to the volcanic aftermath of dry cinders and ash, Maui not only presents a story of volcanic fury, but also the miracle of fertile abundance. It is an awesome story, a tale of birth and change that continues to transform and inspire.

An amau fern (below) takes root in the thin, wind-blown soil trapped between cracks in rock-hardened lava. As ferns establish themselves, their roots help break down the lava rock, creating additional soil and providing a home for still larger plants. The Seven Pools near Hana (left) were formed by the erosive power of a stream cutting its way through accumulated soil into the underlying lava rock.

After West Maui's volcanic fires died, wind and rain carved jagged contours into the curving symmetry of its originally smooth dome. A kukui grove (above) shines in afternoon sunlight falling on portions of West Maui's Olowalu Valley. For uninterrupted eons powerful storms have passed over Maui's volcanic landscape, remaking it in the process. A late afternoon sun (left) shines through clouds at the end of one such storm over Maui's central valley. In the distance, the silhouette of the West Maui Mountains.

Man was linked
to the spiritual world by a diverse
pantheon of gods (above) who were
honored with offerings called
hookipu (right).

Tales of a Demigod

AND AN ISLAND

When the Hawaiians chanted of Maui, they sang of both the demigod and the volcanic island that bore his name, acknowledging each with the mix of familiarity and awe with which the Polynesians interpreted their world. That world, isolated yet self-contained, was dominated by nature and the forces it represented. These in turn were linked to the spiritual world by a diverse pantheon of gods who personified both cosmic and everyday realities.

Chiefly authority came from these gods through ancestral *mana* (spiritual power) acquired at birth, with lineage traced in chants all the way back to the gods themselves. In countless ways man and his gods were part of a continuum that bound the spiritual and physical realms. Ancestral spirits, who lived in a land called Havaiki, were one link in this chain, providing their descendants with access to the spirit world through homage and prayer. The *alii* (royalty) and the demigods were also transitional beings. Just as the *mana*-empowered *alii* were the human transition to the gods, so the demigods were a godly transition to man.

Maui was one of these, a demigod who challenged the gods themselves, and in victory brought man secrets the gods had meant to keep to themselves. Maui the Trickster the Hawaiians affectionately called him, and many *alii* claimed descent from his line. Like Pele, goddess of the volcanic fires, Maui was a great favorite, loved as much for this impetuous bravado as for his deeds and powers.

The people knew of his exploits, related in many chants and stories. One told how he had fished islands from the sea with a hook and line, the origin, some said, of the islands of Hawaii. Other stories told how he had stolen fire from the gods and presented it to man, how he had raised the heavens above the earth, and how he had snared the sun atop Haleakala and, in slowing its transit across the sky, had given man precious extra hours of daylight.

Maui endeared himself to the Hawaiian people. Not only did he lend his name to one of their islands, but he also gave its summit a special place in the tales of ancient Hawaii.

Maui Snares the Sun Atop Haleakala

According to legend, Maui the Trickster was the youngest of four brothers, the children of Akalana and Hina, themselves direct descendants of the great Sky Father, Wakea, and the Earth Mother, Papa.

By some accounts Maui had been magically implanted by a god in Hina's womb, thus endowing him with the burden of an uncertain birthright, a sensitivity to humanity's needs, a rebellious nature, and the talents of a great magician. Like history's other epic heroes, Maui found that he had much to do and much to prove, both to himself and to the gods he dared challenge. In the process he was confronted by many trials, but each time he used trickery to emerge victorious. So it was when Maui set out to capture the sun.

When Hina found that she did not have enough time to dry her tapa cloth, Maui determined to correct the situation by slowing the sun's progress across the heavens. Maui told Hina of his plan to capture the sun and cut off his legs so he could not run so fast. Hina agreed to help him, providing Maui with fifteen strands of twisted fiber. Then she sent him off to find his blind grandmother who lived atop Haleakala where each day she cooked bananas to feed to the sun as he passed overhead.

When he had climbed to the top of Haleakala, Maui found his grandmother by a large *wiliwili* tree about to prepare the sun's bananas. Each time she put one into the pot to cook, Maui removed it until all the bananas were gone.

"Where are the bananas for the sun?" she cried out, sniffing the air to catch a scent of who was bedeviling her. "Who are you? To whom do you belong? Why have you come?" she asked.

"I am Maui. I belong to Hina," Maui replied. "I have come to capture the sun, for he moves too quickly and does not give Hina enough time to dry her tapa cloth."

Hearing this, his grandmother agreed to help, providing Maui with a magic stone for a battle-ax and the final rope required to lasso each of the sun's sixteen legs.

"Make a place to hide by the *wiliwili* tree," she advised. "Then, when the first leg of the sun appears, catch it with your first rope and fasten it to the tree. Then use each of your ropes in the same way until the sun is subdued."

Maui dug himself a hole by the roots of the tree, hiding there until the first rays of the sun appeared. One by one the legs of the sun came over the crater rim and were captured. The sun tried to escape, but Maui held firm, tying him rope by rope to the *wiliwili* tree. When he came after the sun with his magic battle-ax, the sun begged for his life.

"I will spare you if you promise to move more slowly across the sky," Maui replied. Thus humbled, the sun agreed to Maui's terms, to the benefit of Hina and all of Hawaii's people.

*U*sing sixteen strands of rope, Maui captured the legs of the sun as they came over Haleakala's western rim.

Beaches

No matter what else a tropical island offers, it is beaches that help determine just how close to paradise that island is in the popular imagination. Beautiful beaches, in fact, are a key in accounting for Maui's appeal. From secluded crescents bordered by promontories of black lava rock, to longer stretches of beach protected by offshore reefs, Maui provides a wide range of very appealing choices.

For as long as people have inhabited Maui, its coast has played a significant role in providing sustenance and pleasure. So it is today. A visit to just about any of Maui's beaches is likely to prove the point, with swimmers and snorkelers, outrigger canoeists and sailors, surfers and fishermen in evidence from dawn until well after dusk.

As elsewhere, the sea demands caution from those who want to enjoy its refreshing waters. When the surf is high, Maui's beaches can be dangerous, thanks to powerful tides, rip currents, and pounding breakers. If the red flag of caution is up, its message should be taken seriously. Sharp-edged coral and lava rock also provide hazards for the unwary. Cuts received from either are easy to get and take a long time to heal.

From the red sand of Hana's Kaihalulu Beach to Wailea's golden strands, from the reef-sheltered crescent of Kapalua to Kaanapali's expansive stretch of coast, Maui's beaches offer access to waters alive with the brilliance of melted opals at temperatures that range from the heavenly to the sublime. Where to find Maui at its best? Many would head straight to the nearest beach for an answer.

Puu Olai, a
small coastal cinder cone, forms
the northern boundary of Makena,
also known as Big Beach, and
Oneloa ("long sand"). Many
consider Makena to be Maui's finest
beach, its mile of golden sand
fronting marvelous swimming
waters when the surf is low.
Sunbathing on Wailea's Mokapu Beach,
with the island of Kahoolawe lying on
the western horizon. (left)

*The sun-drenched
beaches of Wailea offer many
activities, such as sailing
and windsurfing.*

Kihei's Kamaole Beach faces the distant West Maui mountain range.

Pineapple fields surround West Maui beaches at Makuleia, Fleming Park, and Oneloa In the distance, the villas of the elegant Kapalua Resort.

A portion of one of Kaanapali's two wonderful beaches, seen from Black Rock.

*T*he tail of a giant humpback rises high above the surface of Maui's waters as it prepares to dive. In the background, West Maui canefields.

The Humpback Whale

GIANTS OF THE MAUI SEA

From atop a hundred foot cliff overlooking Maalaea Bay, lustrous royal blue seas stretch toward the horizon. Whitecaps add texture to waters partly enclosed by the nearby islands of Kahoolawe, Molokai, and Lanai, providing a deceptive cover for the giant humpback whales that congregate here each winter to mate, breed, and nurse their young. One false sighting follows another until a vertical plume of water dramatically signals the presence of one of the five to six hundred humpbacks that annually establish themselves in Maui's waters from November through May.

Providing a sanctuary for breeding and nursing in Maui's waters has emerged as an environmental priority. In the meantime, the humpback has been granted full protection by the Marine Mammal Protection and the Endangered Species acts. Injuring or harassing humpbacks in any fashion is strictly forbidden, which means that Maui's whale-watchers must keep their distance in these coastal waters.

Much remains unknown about these great mammals, but research off the Maui coast has begun to answer numerous questions about their habits and has brought to light an array of interesting facts making the endangered humpback all the more intriguing and worthy of respect and protection.

Of the ninety species of whale, humpbacks are one of the largest, weighing in at up to forty-five tons and growing to forty-five feet in length. Even a newborn is of substantial size, birthing at between fifteen hundred and two thousand pounds. Humpbacks are extremely rare. The entire North Pacific herd, of which the Maui humpbacks are members, contains an estimated eight hundred and fifty individuals. Worldwide the total is perhaps between five and seven thousand. Humpbacks were once far more numerous, but whaling in the nineteenth century almost drove them to extinction. It remains uncertain if there is sufficient breeding stock left to save this remarkable species.

A humpback surfaces in a near vertical thrust called spy-hopping, providing it with an opportunity to survey its surroundings. The sun sets over the island of Lanai as a whale-watch cruise returns to port in Lahaina (inset).

© Deborah Glockner-Ferrari

Like certain other mammals, humpbacks don't eat during the mating season. Instead, they live off accumulated fat for somewhere between three and five months, despite the tremendous exertion of migrations that take them from Alaska to Hawaii.

An escort whale almost always accompanies a nursing mother. It was once thought to play a midwife's role, but recent research reveals that these escorts are more likely aggressive males, very possibly awaiting a chance to mate with the female.

The distinctive markings on the underside of the humpback's tail are used to identify individuals, for they are as unique as human fingerprints. A photographic library of these markings is maintained in Seattle by the Department of Commerce through its Marine Fisheries Service.

Humpbacks communicate by one of the most sophisticated language systems in the animal kingdom. The humpback's lyric communication is produced by the transfer of air between pockets within the whale's head, and can be scientifically monitored over distances measured in thousands of miles. Such singing has only been recorded in mating waters, where the same song, varying from day to day, may well by sung by related pods.

Oxygen-breathing mammals, humpbacks can remain submerged no longer than fifteen to twenty minutes. Most dives last three to five minutes, with the return to the surface preceded by air exhaled from a blowhole atop the head at the astonishing rate of three hundred miles per hour. The humpback's most spectacular above-surface exercise is the breaching, when it leaps out of the water before making a dive. Other sightings include spy-hopping, when a humpback surfaces in a near vertical thrust that allows it to survey its surroundings; and fluking, when its back and tail are revealed as it swims near the ocean surface.

Docked in Lahaina Harbor, the *Carthaginian*, the only authentically restored brig in the world, is a scaled-down replica of the masted whaling ships that once anchored off Lahaina's coast. The *Carthaginian* and the museum at Kaanapali's Whalers Village complex both provide an excellent introduction to the humpback, with displays and video documentaries. The humpback also serves as an inspiration for Maui's artists, with painters, sculptors, airbrush artists, potters, and jewelers producing excellent works starring the humpback. Lahaina has become a center for the revival of scrimshaw, the fine art of decorating whale bone or fossil ivory. Maui shops feature examples that range from roughly etched souvenirs to artistic triumphs costing several thousand dollars.

A humpback mother and calf play in waters facing Lahaina in a painting by artist Robert Lyn Nelson. Humpbacks mate, nurse, and train their young in the sheltered waters off the Maui coast from November through May, after traveling thousands of miles from Alaska.

© Robert Lyn Nelson

Remembering an Ancient Heritage

Sometime during the sixth or seventh century, unnamed explorers set out from the Marquesas in double-hulled voyaging canoes on journeys that would take them to the islands of Hawaii. Theirs was a magnificent feat of navigation, matched some five hundred years later by a new wave of settlers who reached Hawaii from Tahiti.

According to tradition, the Tahitians were the first to settle on Maui, choosing the dry south coast of Haleakala, below modern Ulupalakua, as the site for a settlement they called Kahiki Nui, or Great Tahiti. Eventually, as these first Hawaiians prospered, they settled in shoreline fishing villages and in farm villages in Maui's great coastal valleys. It was during this period that a distinctive Hawaiian culture emerged, drawing upon the Polynesian tradition where *alii* (chiefs) and *kahuna* (priests) ruled through clearly defined and strictly enforced prohibitions called *kapu*s. In English the word has reached us as taboo.

These early Mauians lived in houses whose walls were most often made of densely packed *pili* grass tied to a wooden frame. A single low entrance provided access to a sparsely furnished room dominated by a fireplace set into the floor. Plaited mats of the *hala* plant covered portions of the floor, and a deep pile of mats set to one side was used for sleeping. Light was provided by *kukui* nut candles, with supplies and family possessions stored in gourds and woven baskets hung from wall or ceiling hooks.

Cooking was done out of doors, usually in an *imu*, an underground oven that allowed food to be slowly steam-cooked. Life was made easier by a wide variety of finely crafted tools, weapons, and household utensils made of wood, leaves, rock, bone, and shell. Clothing consisted primarily of the *malo*, or loincloth, for men and a long flowing robe for women. *Tapa* cloth, often handstamped with geometric designs, was made of beaten bark strips, with the softest fabric used for bedding. For the *alii*, special feathered cloaks, headdresses, and leis served as symbols of royal authority.

The pigs, dogs, and chickens that were raised for food were supplemented by the sea's abundance and a combination of wild and cultivated plants, most important of which were coconut, taro, yams, and breadfruit. People lived an active life, devoting their free time to a variety of competitive games and sports, including surfing, wrestling, and *konane*, a board game similar to checkers.

The pigs, dogs, and chickens that were raised for food were supplemented by the sea's abundance. A fisherman using a Hawaiian style throw net prepares to check his catch.

It wasn't until the early sixteenth century that Maui was first unified under the rule of a single chief name Piilani. But the dynastic wars that followed Piilani's death were a prelude to similar wars that were to hinder efforts at unification of the island's independent chiefs.

In the late eighteenth century, when high chief Kahekili not only united Maui but also brought Lanai, Molokai, and Oahu under his rule, it seemed a single Hawaiian kingdom under Maui's control might be in the offing. Kahekili's ambitions, however, were complicated by similar designs of chief Kalaniopuu, who along with his sons and warrior nephew Kamehameha had secured control of the Big Island and now wanted to expand his domain.

The ultimate victory belonged to Kamehameha, though it was delayed until 1794 after Kahekili and Kalaniopuu had both died. His opportunity came when Kahekili's heirs turned against each other in a series of wars of succession. At a battle of war canoes along the Kahului coast, followed by pursuit inland to Iao Valley, modern weapons were put to good advantage by Kamehameha, thanks to the support of two Western sailors who had become part of his retinue.

If Maui's independence had been lost, its significance to Kamehameha, his two powerful Maui-born wives, and their offspring soon made Maui the pivotal island of the united archipelago. Fast-changing events soon overwhelmed traditions built up over the centuries. As a new era dawned, it was on Maui, with Lahaina as royal capital, that the future course of events began to unfold.

Hawaii State Archives

King Kamehameha I, called "the great," unified the islands of the Hawaiian archipelago under his rule. His primary rival in this long quest for dominion was Maui High Chief Kahekili. Maui-born Kaahumanu, favorite wife of Kamehameha I, served as regent of the Hawaiian kingdom after Kamehameha's death, guiding the reigns of his sons, Kamehameha II and Kamehameha III.

Amfac Collection — by Herb Kane

*T*he early Mauians lived in houses whose walls were most often made of densely packed pili grass tied to a wooden frame, with a single low entrance providing access. Life was made easier by a wide variety of finely crafted tools and utensils made of wood, leaves, rock, bone, and shell. A weaver crafts a basket of hala leaves in traditional Hawaiian style.

Hawaii State Archives

Lahaina

WHALING CAPITAL OF THE WORLD

When the first missionaries arrived on Maui in 1823, they came ashore to a large Polynesian village of coconut palms and thatch huts. Their landfall was Lahaina, named, some say, for the merciless sun *(la haina)* that still beats down on many an afternoon. Long a playground for Maui's *alii*, Lahaina had become Hawaii's de facto capital, thanks to a central location in the midst of the recently unified Hawaiian archipelago, ready access to the sea, and fertile lowlands brought to life by ample fresh water diverted from West Maui's mountainous interior. Before Lahaina lost its preeminence as a port of call to Honolulu's magnificent deep-water harbor, it would serve as a mid-Pacific crossroads for four historic and tumultuous decades.

The American missionaries who settled Maui came to establish "an elevated state of Christian civilization," bringing with them not only the gospels and a new moral order, but the secular schooling required to introduce the Hawaiians to the technology, economics, and ideas of the nineteenth-century Western world.

Their aims were frustrated by the growing number of whalers and sailors who were given shore leave for hell-bent bouts of "rest and recreation" while their ships were reprovisioned after months, and sometimes years at sea. "What a happy discovery these islands were," a crewman on one ship noted. "What would the American trade be without them to winter at and get every refreshment?"

That reality wasn't lost on Lahaina, with its abundance of goods ranging from yams to pork, from salt to fresh water. In time, as trade and whaling developed,

Hawaii State Archives

Picturesque
Lahaina harbor at sunset.
Nineteenth-century whalers
pursue their prey (lower left)

even Maui's people would become articles of commerce. Many of the men signed on as sailors, while the women, along with the grog shops that opened along Front Street, provided ship-weary crews with readily available pleasures. By the 1840s, with Lahaina emerging as the whaling capital of the world, local authorities and their missionary allies found themselves in open conflict with growing numbers of exceedingly boisterous sailors doing their best to give meaning to the slogan "No God West of the Horn."

But time and circumstance would resolve the problem far better than missionary sermons. By the 1860s, with the capital already moved to Honolulu and the days of commercial whaling numbered, Lahaina drifted from the mainstream to the periphery, spending close to a century as a sugarcane plantation town servicing West Maui canefields and the Pioneer Mill.

Thanks to the grass roots efforts of the Lahaina Restoration Foundation, Lahaina awoke from its Van Winkle-esque slumber in time to preserve much of what remained of its past. While some consider the result too commercialized, for most Lahaina retains its unique character, benefitting from masterful restorations of a number of important historic buildings that have been opened to the public.

Today, despite the considerable development that has transformed much of the nearby coast into Hawaii's most popular destination outside of Waikiki, Lahaina remains a small town meant for walking. Major attractions are found within minutes of one another, including the Baldwin Mission House (1836), where medical missionary Dwight Baldwin lived with his family; Hale Paahao, the old prison, literally translated as "stuck-in-irons-house"; the Wo Hing Society Hall (1912), with its displays on Chinese culture; Hale Pai (1836), the printing house where some of the first books printed in the islands were produced; and the brig *Carthaginian*, with its on-board museum on humpback whales.

If Front Street once bustled with the noise of sailors on leave, today it caters to a mix of locals and visitors, each taking in the passing scene. Shopping and dining are the main attractions, with a range of specialty shops, galleries, and restaurants housed in the renovated and rebuilt plantation-era stores that line both sides of the street. The commercial stretch of Front Street is protected as one of two County-legislated historic districts. The second is centered on Banyan Square, a shaded acre that provides Lahaina with a harbor-front park. The Pioneer Inn, built in 1901 and now Hawaii's oldest hotel, is one of several historic buildings bordering the square.

It is this combination of historically significant buildings and architectural charm that makes Lahaina more than just a caricature, for beneath the surface is a community committed to maintaining its historic integrity, and along with it, Lahaina's unusual blend of the casual and the sophisticated.

Canefields cover the West Maui lowlands lying between Lahaina and the sawtooth West Maui Mountains. In the mid—nineteenth century these same fields provided supplies to reprovision hundreds of sailing ships and whalers each year.

A *group of nineteenth-century whalers grace a fossil scrimshaw-cut walrus tooth (above left). The Baldwin Mission House (above right), built in 1836, was the first of Lahaina's historic buildings to be restored and opened to the public. Built in 1901, the Pioneer Inn (top right) is Hawaii's oldest hotel.*

L *ahaina harbor attracts a fleet of pleasure craft, many of which offer daily sails in coastal waters (lower left). Lahaina as a nineteenth-century plantation town (lower right).*

47

Canefields sprawl over the Maui landscape. Flowering sugarcane (inset).

Sugar's Reign as King

To the Hawaiians, the tall grass we call sugarcane was known as *ko*. A traditional part of the Hawaiian diet, it was one of the plants the first Hawaiians brought with them from the South Pacific, planting it in clumps where the soil was good and water plentiful. Planted next to homes, its tall stalks, often growing to heights of fifteen to twenty feet, were cut and chewed for their sweet juice.

As early as 1828 two Chinese merchants had taken advantage of Maui's ample supply of wild cane to refine sugar in Wailuku. It wasn't until the middle of the century, however, as whaling's ultimate decline became obvious, that sugar came to be considered an alternative capable of providing comparable economic stability for Maui.

By the 1860s, thanks to demand created by events such as the California gold rush and the American Civil War, when Hawaiian supplies replaced traditional sources for portions of the American market, sugar plantations and mills were in operation all over Maui. Designed to be virtually self-sufficient, Hawaii's plantations were company towns, employing an assortment of immigrants brought in from all over the world to compensate for Hawaii's declining population.

The native Hawaiians in fact were in desperate straits, succumbing to illness and losing the will to live in numbers that seriously threatened them with extinction as a people. For sugar to prosper as a commercial crop required a ready labor supply, which meant importing contract laborers from China, Japan, Puerto Rico, the Portuguese Azores, Korea, and the Philippines.

"The decrease in our population," Kamehameha IV told the Hawaiian legislature in 1855, "is a subject in comparison to which all others sink into insignificance." By 1864 the problem had gotten worse instead of better, despite government efforts to revitalize the Hawaiian stock by settling other Pacific Islanders in Hawaii.

"The wants of our agriculture, the dictates of humanity and the preservation of our race demand that the Government should control this operation," Kamehameha V stated in creating the Bureau of Immigration. In 1865, 522 contract laborers were brought in from Hong Kong to be sent to work Hawaii's plantations, including those on Maui. Three years later the first Japanese arrived, and the decades that followed saw

Hawaii's immigrant population swell, with almost all its newly acquired citizens employed in plantation agriculture.

The history of sugar on Maui is the story of these immigrants and the ways in which they came to redefine Hawaii. It is also the story of unusual individuals who had the foresight and entrepreneurial skill to make Maui's sugar industry one of the world's most efficient and modern. They were men like Claus Spreckels, a California millionaire planter who established himself on Maui in 1876, and within a decade not only controlled the island's economy, but had become an advisor to the King and others of the *alii*.

In time Spreckels lost control of his sugar empire to the businessmen sons of Maui's first missionary families. They labored to assure sugar's dominance well into the middle of the twentieth century.

Today sugar and pineapple continue to play an important role on Maui, as tens of thousands of well-cultivated acres reveal. Other crops have been added to the Maui harvest in the past decade, including exotic protea blossoms from upcountry nurseries and recently planted groves of macadamia nut trees.

Agriculture may no longer be king on Maui, and the days of the plantation may well be over, but sugar and pineapple remain fundamental ingredients of the present and will continue to play a vital role in Maui's transition from one era to another.

__A__ ripe pineapple ready for harvest in a Kapalua field. Pineapple harvesting (bottom below). A canefield is set on fire to burn off leaves, allowing for easier harvest and transport to the mill. Several mills still operate on Maui, but none are open to the public.

*S*unrise atop
Haleakala . . . winter's chill in
the tropics.

Haleakala

MAGIC ABOVE THE CLOUDS

Rising nearly six miles from the ocean floor, the serrated edge of Haleakala's summit passes through the clouds to scrape the tropic sky. Well past the tree line the summit crater's encompassing walls face the heavens like a huge eye on the universe. Within its confines lie vivid cinder cones, fields of volcanic ash, acres of sweet-smelling grasses, and an abundance of secrets that are the true measure of its power to inspire.

In ancient times a *heiau* (temple) stood atop the crest of Haleakala's eastern rim, providing access to the gods and a vantage for panoramas that remain unchanged. To the southeast, the curving silhouettes of Mauna Kea and Mauna Loa float above the hundred-mile-wide sea of water and clouds that separate them from Haleakala. To the north, twenty-one miles of towering rock wall encircle the crater floor some two thousand feet below. What lies before you is the largest dormant volcanic crater in the world, now protected as Haleakala National Park.

Silence and wind seem to echo through this huge hollow, often carrying with them massed armies of billowing clouds that flow through two cracks in the crater wall. Kaupo and Koolau, as these gaps are called, reveal one of the epic changes that time and again have transformed this great volcanic mountain.

The ever-present evidence of past eruptions seems an incongruous contrast to this vast, silent, immobile crater. Only the shadows of clouds, the chill

gusts of high-altitude winds and the sudden appearance of a solitary insect or bird seem to move. While days are often unrelentingly hot in the crater below, it can be chilly at summit lookouts, particularly when the sun is blocked by clouds or has passed below the horizon.

The concentration of cinders and ash that gives the western half of Haleakala a lunar appearance also offers the most popular access route to the crater floor. Keoneheehee, "the sliding sands," the Hawaiians called this serpentine descent, and the name is as appropriate today as it was in Polynesian times when the crater was used as a route linking central Maui with Hana. What makes a visit a lot easier today are three National Park cabins that allow for a circuit of the crater floor in daily hikes of from three to ten miles.

For those who prefer to explore on horseback, there are several escorted options providing ever-changing views of the magnificent interior and its distinctive flora and fauna. Highlights are the flowering Silverswords (an exotic relative of the sunflower found only on Haleakala's summit) and the flightless Nene goose, a native Hawaiian cousin of the Canada goose that was, until recently, on the verge of extinction.

When it comes to the unusual, nature hasn't limited its efforts to the tangible atop Haleakala. If conditions are right, a natural phenomenon known as the Spectre of the Brocken can be seen when the setting sun shines through misting clouds to create a circular rainbow on the denser clouds in the crater below. If you're standing between the setting sun and the clouds, it is your shadow that will appear in the center of the rainbow. This shadowy figure is the Spectre of the Brocken.

More than the Spectre of the Brocken makes the end of day atop Haleakala worthwhile. About an hour before sunset, with most of the crater in shadow, the constant flow of visitors diminishes to a trickle. In the distance West Maui lies capped in clouds that absorb the electric colors of the setting sun, subduing them to rich pastels in the process. A bit to the south, Lanai lies awash in a golden ocean, then turns amber as the sun passes from view. Each day the scenario changes, with only the intensity of the moment providing a common denominator.

Yet it is the sunrise not the sunset that receives the lion's share of recognition and acclaim. Perhaps it is the sense of adventure in a 3 A.M. departure from Maui's coastal resorts and the ride to the summit in the predawn darkness that provide the sunrise with the impact of a unique experience.

It is best to arrive while the night sky still dominates, giving new meaning to the path of stars called the Milky Way. As the stars disappear, a ribbon of brilliant color brightens the eastern horizon, announcing the sun's imminent return. Then, as on the mythical day when the demigod Maui sat in wait with the sun as his prey, its starburst rays clear the crater rim. In silent exhilaration another day of magic above the clouds has begun.

"If you're standing between the setting sun and the clouds, it is your shadow that will appear in the center of the rainbow. This shadowy figure is the Spectre of the Brocken." A Nene goose and a flowering Silversword, two unique residents of Haleakala crater.

Well past the tree line, Haleakala's encompassing walls face the heavens like a huge eye on the universe.

The winding road to Hana offers a breathtaking view.

Hana

ONE VIEW OF PARADISE

For some, Hana is the ultimate paradise. On a brilliantly vibrant day color rushes at you in profound abundance. The earth glows with the lush greens of forest and pasture stitched to a royal blue sea by white waves crashing on black lava rock.

A glorious sky, alive with billowing clouds, overhangs waterfalls that race toward the sea. From the air you can trace them to their source, up a staircase of pools, cascades, and cataracts that drain the cloud-banked northeast slopes of Haleakala. This is Hana, or more correctly, the stretch of Maui coast that winds from Keanae to Kaupo, with the town of Hana at its center.

Some would say that Hana's influence, the impact of family ties, land ownership, and lifestyle, now reaches from Ulupalakua to Paia. It's a large portion of Maui, linked by a rural orientation, Hawaiian spirit, and a very evident pride in being peripheral to the mainstream. In this sense, Hana is more than a place, for it represents a way of life that is Polynesian at its core — sensual, sensitive, and languorous, yet ultimately down to earth and practical.

Time moves at a leisurely pace, and that's the way people want it. More than fifty miles of dips and curves, cliff-hanging ascents, and one-lane bridges link Hana to the outside world at Paia. It's not an easy drive. The options are flying into Hana's tiny airstrip or the long ride in on a partly paved road from Ulupalakua, but the Hana road is the real lifeline. People are very conscious of how isolation adds to a sense of community. It is something they take seriously. When a referendum for a major road upgrade was held some years ago it was defeated. Better to let the road serve as a buffer between Hana and the outside world.

Today ranching dominates in Hana. Once it was sugar, but isolation made that unprofitable and pasture replaced canefields. Hana remains a company town however, dominated by the Hana Ranch. Few seem to complain, for the Ranch pursues its operations with the welfare of the community very obviously in mind.

It's the overall setting and slow pace that have established Hana's credentials as a fragment of paradise. Charles Lindbergh thought enough of Hana to settle there (he is buried on the grounds of a small Kipahulu church), and other notables, including Carol Burnett and George Harrison, have also chosen Hana as a retreat. There are highlights, of course. The water-filled caves and tidal pools as Waianapanapa, the view from the Keanae

Fields of taro cover the Keanae Peninsula halfway to Hana on the coastal road (upper left). A farmer tends a field of taro near Kipahulu (lower left). An Avocado and torch ginger grow in a Hana garden. (right)

Lookout, or from the cross that overlooks Hana town, the diverse array of goods and customers at the Hasegawa General Store, and numerous waterfall-fed pools framed by tropical vegetation are all part of Hana's soothing magic.

Superlatives are the very nature of Hana's appeal. No single visit captures all its charms, for they are as varied as the flow of time and circumstance. Hana's impact may be felt in the rattling of giant bamboo shaken by gentle tradewinds, in the less-than-subtle assault of brilliant colors in a coastal panorama, or through a smile that inspires with its warmth and clarity. Yes, Hana is more than a place, it's a frame of mind and the secret of discovery comes in just being there.

Ripening mangoes.
*The town of Hana lies nestled
between the large bay from which it
takes its name, and the verdant
hillsides of the Hana Ranch.
Hana Papayas. (below)*

***A** diver tosses a lei into the surf from Kaanapali's Black Rock.*